# 8 Steps to Helping Your Child in School

## The Parents' Guide to Working with Their Child at Home

**Strategies to Improve Your Child's Academic Skills**

*by*

**Dr. Alicia Holland**

This book may be ordered through booksellers or by contacting:

iGlobal Educational Services, LLC
13785 Highway 183, Suite 125
Austin, Texas 78750
www.iglobaleducation.com
512-761-5898

Because of the dynamic nature of the Internet, any web addresses or links contained in this book may have changed since publication and may no longer be valid. The views expressed in this work are solely those of the author and do not necessarily reflect the views of the publisher, and the publisher hereby disclaims any responsibility for them.

This is a work of fiction. Names, characters, businesses, places, events, and incidents are either the products of the author's imagination or used in a fictitious manner. Any resemblance to actual persons, living or dead, or actual events is purely coincidental.

8 Steps to Helping Your Child in School

ISBN-13: 978-1-944346-08-9

# Dedication

I dedicate this to all parents. You have a special role in helping your children on their life and spiritual journey. Remember, you are loved, valued, and competent.

# Table of Contents

# Introduction

Maybe you are already homeschooling your child or you have decided that you need to spend more time with your child to ensure that he or she is learning to his or her full potential. Perhaps, your child may be enrolled in a public or private school and you may be supplementing your child's education with a tutor, along with helping your child at home.

Whatever the case may be, this book is going to take you on a journey that will only help both you and your child grow and learn together. Most importantly, you will have the skills necessary to feel confident about teaching your own child.

Knowing how to help your child can be a challenge. I know this from both personal and professional experiences. I'm a professional tutor, public school educator, online professor, and a mother who works with both adults and children. Most importantly, I have the luxury of helping my personal children at home with their studies and have put these practices into place with them.

You probably have a working knowledge of how to work with your child at home, but you need good information to help you strategically implement a plan to get the highest results. My goal with this book is to provide you with this information and I truly believe that my perspective, as a mother with a strong educational background, can help you.

You don't have to read this book from the first page to the last—although you can. You may want to read the first part to get an understanding of how you should get to know your child and then move on to the other parts that may fit your current needs.

# My Assumptions

In order to provide you with material to meet your unique situation, I had to make some basic assumptions. I assume the following:

1. You have a desire to spend time with your child on his or her studies.
2. You want information on how to help your child succeed academically.

# How This Book
# is Organized

8 *Steps to Helping Your Child in School: The Parents'*
*Guide to Working with their Child at Home* is divided
into eight parts that will address how to monitor your
child's progress.

### Step One: Getting to Know Your Child...
### Academically

You may already know what your child likes or what your
child would do on a typical Saturday, but do you know what
your child is capable of achieving...academically? This step
will help you understand your child better. If you feel like it,
you should try to use this step to discover your own learning
style and multiple intelligences. The more you know about
yourself and your child, the better!

## Step Two: Choosing the Right Environment for Your Child to Complete Homework or Work on School-Related Materials.

What should you put in your child's workspace? Does your child need one? This step details what you need to have available at all times in your child's workspace and highlights why your child needs a private, personal workspace other than the kitchen table. The more ownership that your child senses in having a workspace, the more pride they will have when completing homework or learning activities at home.

## Step Three: Selecting a Curriculum for Your Child

Do you already have a curriculum or will you need to purchase one? For this step, you will learn how to strategically choose curriculum that really meets your child's needs and not the store you bought it from. There are five must-read questions that you must consider when selecting curriculum for your child. These strategies can be applied whether your child attends school or is homeschooled.

## Step Four: Planning Your Child's Lessons

Planning your child's lessons is more than printing out a worksheet. It does take a little more effort to make sure that your child is learning the concepts that he or she truly needs assistance with in school. In this step, you are going to learn what you need to begin the lesson planning process and how to plan lessons for your child. What if you do not have time to plan lessons? Well, this step covers that information too!

## Step Five: Supplementing Your Child's Curriculum

After you have tried everything that you know how to, your child still does not get it. What's a parent to do? In this step, you will learn various outlets for supplementing your child's curriculum or homework such as finding tutors and online resources to help you with your child. Imagine that!

## Step Six: Assessing Your Child's Progress

How do you know if your child got it? This step discusses many types of assessments and provide several examples of how these types of assessments may be used. In addition, it includes information on how to find quality assessments that are rigorous and help with problem-solving skills.

## Step Seven: Reporting Your Child's Grades and Keeping Records

How do you justify what you are teaching your child? How do know what has been covered or how well your child did on a lesson? It's easy…keep track of your child's progress. This step discusses two strategies you can use to keep track of your child's records and help him or her grow even more.

## Step Eight: Professional Development for ME, the Parent

This step offers resources within the community that parents may want to research or consider joining.

*Step*

# 1

# Getting to Know Your Child...Academically.

You may already know what your child likes or dislikes because you have spent the most time with your child over the course of his or her life. As a result, you have valuable information outside of academics that can help your child succeed. Here are two questions to help you get started with getting to know your child:

1. What have you noticed about your child's likes and dislikes?

   _____

   _____

   _____

   _____

   _____

   _____

   _____

**2.** What are your child's strengths and weaknesses?

_____

_____

_____

_____

_____

_____

_____

Before you can begin to help your child academically, you will need to conduct several assessments that will provide valuable information about your child. We will discuss these assessments, but first we need to cover a few terms. These terms are: (a) learning style; and (b) multiple intelligences.

What is a learning style? A learning style is "an individual's mode of gaining knowledge" (Dictionary.com, 2010). In other words, it is the way that he or she likes to learn new materials. Neil Fleming found four different learning styles:

(a) visual
(b) auditory
(c) kinesthetic
(d) tactile

The *visual learning style* allows the learner to use pictures, graphics, or other visual images to construct meaning of new knowledge that he or she may be learning. Examples of visuals that can be used to help reinforce concepts are posters, video clips, drawings, or graphic organizers. Let's imagine that you are helping your child with adding and subtracting numbers. You could use objects around the house, such as paper clips, marbles, or buttons to help him or her understand how to add and subtract numbers or you may choose to use homemade visuals. In my experience as both a teacher and tutor, I have found that children do well with both, but they seem to take ownership of a visual that they have constructed.

The *auditory learning style* allows the learner to listen to information to learn new information. For example, children who prefer this learning style would enjoy listening to someone read, talk about a topic, or explain how to do something. Children already use this learning style when learning how to pick up new language whether it is at home or at school.

The *kinesthetic learning* style allows the learner to move freely to construct meaning from new information. For instance, children who love to act out a situation or play with their friends are learning. This is why it is so important for parents to allow their children to play outside or in general. Believe it or not, your child is learning and having fun at the same time. Examples of kinesthetic activities include singing, dancing, and moving the body freely.

The *tactile learning style* allows the learner to use hands and fingers to manipulate an object to better understand a topic. This learning style is highly used with today's children since they are constantly on the computer playing games online. They are educational and provide a fun atmosphere to help them learn information.

Why do you need to know about your child's learning style? This information will help you plan lessons or help your child complete his or her homework. For example, your child may like to learn by doing things hands-on. Learning activities should be centered on how he or she likes to learn.

If you are looking for more information on these learning styles, you can just do an Internet search.

Now that you have been introduced to the different learning styles, it is time to take a closer look at Howard Gardner's Multiple Intelligences.

Did you know that everyone is born with unique talents? I like to say that everyone has a purpose and should at least get some insight into what that purpose may be. A way for parents to tap into a child's skills and ability is to assess their multiple intelligences. According to Microsoft Network (MSN) Encarta Dictionary (2010), "Multiple intelligences are several independent forms of human intelligence that exist, according to one psychological theorist, Howard Gardner" (¶2). In other words, every human has different types of intelligences that make him or her the person that he or she is.

Below are ten multiple intelligences that are found in humans:

| Intelligence type | Capability and perception |
|---|---|
| Linguistic | words and language |
| Logical-Mathematical | logic and numbers |
| Musical | music, sound, rhythm |
| Bodily-Kinesthetic | body movement control |
| Spatial-Visual | images and space |
| Interpersonal | other people's feelings |
| Intrapersonal | self-awareness |
| Naturalist | natural environment |
| Spiritual/Existential | religion and 'ultimate issues' |
| Moral | ethics, humanity, value of life |

(Businessballs.com, 2010)

Why do I need to know about Howard Gardner's Multiple Intelligences? These multiple intelligences can help you and your child plan his or her future based upon knowing what he or she is good at. For example, think about celebrities. What multiple intelligences do they possess? At a young age, most of them knew what their talents and multiple intelligences were so throughout their school years they capitalized on that information.

Where can you find a free multiple intelligence question-naire for your child? There are several more resources that you can use to find out your child's multiple intelligences located on the resource page. You will find several links that will give you and your child the opportunity to take an online multiple intelligence assessment or print one out, if you wish.

After you have explored how your child prefers to learn and the different ways your child learns, it's time to choose the right spot for him or her to work on homework or school stuff.

# Choosing the Right Environment for Your Child to Complete Homework or Work on School-Related Materials.

You have just learned about how your child likes to learn. Now, it's time to choose a quiet location in the house to help him or her complete homework or other school-related tasks. Right now, you may be using the kitchen table as his or her desk or you may be using it as the classroom. No matter how you are using it, it is very important to move your child to a quieter and stable location in the house.

This area does not have to be huge, but it does need to be an area where your child can always go to work. This might be an area where he or she may be comfortable reading or writing. Also, this area needs to be dedicated to only one purpose. That way learning materials can be left and readily available when your child is ready to begin working on his or her assignments.

What should be placed in this space? Please make sure that you have the following available at all times:

1.  **School Supplies:** Make sure that pencils, pens, paper, and other supplies are available so that your child does not waste time looking for these materials.

2.  **Desk/Table and Chair:** You may opt to include a small table with a chair or a student desk. These can be found at a bargain store or you may find quality furniture on your city's craigslist. It's important that your child is able to sit up straight and focus rather than lying down to complete his or her work. Besides, your child is able to save his or her back in the process.

3.  **Notepads/Dry Erase Boards:** You may want to purchase some sticky notes or mini dry erase boards to show examples to your child. Walgreen's or Target has mini-dry erase boards at a reasonable price. If you want ten or so dry-erase boards to share with other parents or your child's friends, you can buy a sheet of white panel at Home Depot and have them cut it into 3 x 5 or whatever size you desire. This is the cheapest route, but again, this depends on what you want to do.

4. **Computer with Guidelines:** Let's face it—a computer is a part of every child's life. In today's society, students use the computer for many different things, such as finding additional information or composing an assignment. During homework time, you can use the Internet to get help on some homework. I will be discussing more about how to supplement your child's homework or curriculum in Step 5.

 Don't forget to set computer guidelines because the Internet can be a dangerous place and children should be taught how to use the computer appropriately. For a sample family internet pledge, you should be able to find one on the Internet for a nominal fee or maybe for free.

5. **Printer/Scanner:** You and your child will need to print assignments or information that you have found on the Internet. Therefore, you will need a printer in this workspace. If you are thinking about purchasing a printer, you should make sure that it has combined features, such as the ability to scan, copy, fax, and print. This is the best value for your buck and you will be happy with your purchase.

6. **Organizers:** The workspace should have organizers, such as shelves to put binders or notebooks in an organized manner. Often times, children keep their learning activities from year to year and need a system to

help stay organized. A good place to get cheap, but quality organizers would be at discount stores, such as Wal-Mart, Ross's, Goodwill, or Target. It depends on what you want to do and how you would like to accessorize your child's workspace.

7. **Calendar:** Your child should have either a wall calendar or desk calendar, in addition to a school agenda to keep up with learning and family activities. The school agenda should be used solely for school-related matters, but the other calendar could be dedicated to family activities and important dates from school, such as due dates for projects. This will help them get into the habit of using a calendar to plan.

These items listed should be included to have a successful workspace for your child. Below is a quote that helps explain the importance of having a designated place so that your child can reap the benefits of having a workspace.

> **Success is the sum of small efforts, repeated day in and day out.**
>
> — Robert Collier

# Selecting a Curriculum for Your Child

S electing a curriculum for your child can be a hassle if you are not aware of what is out there. Before you can select any curriculum, you need to know why you are looking for it. Here are some questions that can help guide your choice in finding a curriculum to meet your child's needs. They are the following:

1. Do you want to give your child practice on a certain topic? If so, what type of practice (i.e. skill and drill or word problems)?

_____

_____

_____

_____

_____

**2.** Are you looking for Christian-based sources? Is this important to you? If you are looking for Christian-based sources, then how will you make sure that your child can apply critical thinking skills?

_____

_____

_____

_____

_____

_____

**3.** Do you have a budget for finding curriculum? Explain.

_____

_____

_____

_____

_____

_____

The answers that you provide to these three questions will definitely influence the types of curriculum that you may purchase or find for free.

If you are homeschooling or supplementing your child's school work, you should know that there are a set of questions that should be considered when looking for curriculum for your child. To be exact, there are five questions for selecting a curriculum. These questions are the following:

1. **Does it provide the content that my child needs?** This question simply asks if the information is relevant to your child's learning needs. For example, if your child is working on the water cycle, you want to make sure that the curriculum covers the water cycle and possibly a little bit more.

2. **Is it research-based?** This question asks if the curriculum has been proven to be effective with students. In other words, which instructional strategies are being used and are these strategies effective? For instance, a learning activity that requires students to create a visual or graphic organizer for information about the three branches of government would be considered research-based because students must summarize and have a deep understanding of how to put the information into a graphic organizer.

3. **Is it rigorous?** This question really wants to know if the learning activities have students use higher thinking skills. These higher thinking skills could be applying the information in new situations, evaluating, or

problem-solving. This is the level that we want our future to function so that they can have the ability to look at any situation.

4. **Is it real-world or problem-based?** This question wants to know if your child is using the information for more than skill-and-drill. How is your child applying the information? Can he or she relate to the information?

5. **Does the curriculum seem engaging and interactive?** This question wants you to determine if the curriculum have lessons that would engage your child and/or be interactive. Children will have a harder time learning information if it seems boring to them. Therefore, it is in their best interest for you to find engaging and interactive learning activities.

Let's look at two examples about geometry. One example shows a rigorous, real-world, and engaging learning activity, while the other example does not show these characteristics. It is a lower level activity that does not require children to think a little more.

## EXAMPLE 1: "Geometry in the Real World"

# Geometry in the Real World

You are trying to create a picture book of geometry that can be found in our world. In your book, you need to include the following:

- ✓ At least 20 vocabulary terms from the list below.
- ✓ All pictures must be labeled and you should highlight or outline the part of the picture that illustrates the vocabulary term.
- ✓ The book must have a title page, with your name and date.
- ✓ The book must be in some type of cover or folder.

You may need to research some of the terms to find out what they mean. You may use the internet or dictionary.

## Geometry Terms:

1. Square
2. Quadrilateral
3. Parallel lines
4. Hexagon
5. Right Angle
6. Complementary Angles
7. Obtuse Triangle
8. Acute Triangle
9. Skew Lines
10. Trapezoid

### EXAMPLE 2: "Where's my Angle?"

Please answer the following questions.

1. What is an angle?
2. What is the definition of a ray?
3. What is the definition of a square?

What do you think about these two examples? Which one would you want your child to complete? These are two questions that should come up often when selecting any curriculum or resource for your child to work on at home.

Is there one curriculum better than the other? Please understand that you have to use the five questions outlined above to determine if a curriculum fits your child's learning needs. Also, commercial-resources are not always as rigorous as they should be. Therefore, it would be in your child's best interest to find resources that require higher-thinking skills. If you can afford it, hire a certified teacher to write curriculum or tests for you. You can find help by posting an ad on your city's craigslist.

The bottom line is that selecting the right curriculum can make a difference and using the aforementioned questions can help you and your children have meaningful, learning experiences. So, be choosy...your child deserves it.

> If you don't know where you are going,
> you'll end up someplace else.
>
> — Yogi Berra

# Planning Your Child's Lesson

The time has come to put resources together to teach your child. Are you ready? Before you plan any lessons, you should have the following in your possession:

1. **Learning Standards.** The learning standards are used to help you plan which areas and topics your child will need to cover. Depending on your state, these standards are often called state standards and can be found on your state's educational agency website. In some states, the learning standards are called Common Core Standards.

   If you are working from a Christian-based curriculum, I highly recommend that you supplement it with either your state's learning standards or the common core standards. At some point in your child's life, he or she will have to still learn some of the content covered in classrooms across the world to compete in the global economy and carryout daily life skills.

2. **Access to the Internet.** The Internet is actually your friend. There are many educational resources available online to help you with planning your child's lessons. What does the Internet have to do with planning? The Internet can help you find learning activities that are aligned to the learning standards and suitable for your child's learning needs.

3. **Educational Resources.** You may have some print educational resources that you have used over the years or have recently purchased. Whatever resources you use, please make sure that you have it to plan your child's lesson(s).

4. **Planning Book.** You may not like to write (or type), but it is very important to track what your child is learning on a daily basis. As you would want your child's teacher to know and have lesson plans in place to teach, the same expectation should apply to you. There are stores that have planning books available. For example, you need to see if the store has a section dedicated with many teacher resources for educators and parents. This is a great place to start collecting and building your educational resources to help your child at home.

The planning book will be used to write down lesson standards, learning activities, and assessments so that you can keep track of your child's educational needs.

5. **Specific Learning Needs.** You will need to take the information that you have collected in Step One to help you plan lessons for your child. If you know or your child tells you that he or she is not able to do a certain concept, then you should definitely include this information when making lesson plans.

Once you have these in your possession, it's time to go through the curriculum planning phase.

Is there a lesson plan template available for use?

There are several lesson plan templates available, but you want to make sure that this template has everything that you will need to adequately plan for your child's lessons.

My personal favorite is "Madeline Hunter's Model" because it really makes you think about HOW you are going to deliver the lesson. In other words, most of your legwork is done for you.

Madeline Hunter, a well-respected college professor of educational administration and teacher education, developed several noteworthy instructional models in education (Math and Reading Help, 2010).

"Madeline Hunter's Model" includes the following components:

> ➤ **Standards and Lesson Objective:** This information should be listed at the very beginning of each lesson. Questions such as "What will the student learn? What will the learner demonstrate?" are placed here (Math & Science Help, 2010). In other words, these questions will help you craft lesson objective(s) and you should be using the lesson standards to make sure that your child is learning the correct material.

> ➤ **Anticipatory Set:** This is often used as "the hook" to get children interested in the lesson (Math & Science Help, 2010). For example, if you are teaching a lesson over geometry, you would want to ask where they have seen rectangles or parallel lines in their environment. This simple question will spark all sorts of conversations that are really about the topic—geometry. Imagine that!

> ➤ **Teaching/Instructional Process:** This part focuses on the instructional methods that you will use to help your child, such as providing input, modeling, and checking for understanding (Math & Science Help, 2010). This is the meat of your lesson plan and you should list or briefly describe how you will teach your child.

➤ **Guided Practice and Monitoring:** How will you know if your child understands the skill taught? This part of the lesson allows you to ask questions or monitor understanding (Math & Science Help, 2010). The bottom line is that you get to ask your child to explain how he or she understands the information.

➤ **Closure:** When closing a lesson, you want to make sure that you use statements or actions that will help your child make sense out of what he or she has been taught (Math & Science Help, 2010). There are many ways that this can be done and we will discuss this in Step 6.

➤ **Independent Practice:** How do you know if your child can do the work on his or her own? Well, this part of the lesson is designed for your child to answer questions or solve problems that reinforce and extend the learning beyond the actual lesson (Math & Science Help, 2010). In other words, this is where the word problems come into play that provide a real-world context that the child may or may not experience.

# WHAT ELSE DO YOU NEED TO FOCUS ON WHEN PLANNING LESSONS FOR YOUR CHILD?

While Madeline Hunter's Model will definitely help craft a well-designed lesson plan, it is equally important to focus on the following: (a) the lesson objective; (b) lesson activities; (c) assessment; (d) homework; (e) early finisher; and (f) reteaching.

> ➤ **Communicate the Lesson Objective:** This is the most important point of the lesson for your child. It is crucial to put the lesson objective in a kid-friendly way so that they can understand what you are teaching them. For instance, if it is a lesson on comparing and ordering fractions, then you could communicate the lesson objective the following way:

*Today we are learning to compare and order fractions.*

This simple sentence does not veer from the lesson objective and it is language your child can understand. Let's face it—one day (and one day soon) he or she will have to recognize and apply this skill in either a lesson that you teach or in his or her daily life.

> ➤ **Lesson Activities:** Are you using interactive lessons from the Internet or hands-on lessons? It does not matter which lesson activities you use because you are only writing down this information in your lesson plan

so that you can find it later. Have you ever seen or tried something, only to forget where you saw it or got it from? Well, this happens when teaching too! So, please be sure that you have recorded the information.

➤ **Assessment:** How are you going to assess whether your child has learned or not? It may be a wise idea to think about this at the beginning of your lesson. A good place to start is with the learning standard specified for the lesson. Your assessment should match the level your child is expected to apply the information learned from the lesson.

➤ **Homework:** You should assign your child homework, but don't overwhelm them. (No more than 10 word problems at a time in math, for example.) If you decide to assign a project, then it is important that the child know the project requirements. However, they should be broken down in manageable increments.

If your child attends school, he or she should have homework. The amount of homework each day depends on the teacher.

➤ **Early Finisher:** What if your child finishes everything quicker than you expect? This would be a great time to add an activity that allows him or her to show what they know. For example, you could extend the lesson into a writing skill by having him or her write a letter to a friend about how to do the skill.

➤ **Reteaching:** What should you do if your child did not get it the first time around? If you are asking yourself questions as such, then you need to try a different way of teaching the material. This can definitely get tricky, but it can be done. My advice to you is to use the learning styles information from Step One to see how your child likes to learn.

It's so easy to start teaching because either your child or you are interested. Whether you are homeschooling your child or working with your child at home over the summer or during the school year, you need to have a plan in place. Don't forget to add fun to your lessons so that your child can be engaged.

> **People don't plan to fail; they fail to plan.**
> — Harvey MacKay

## Step

# 5

# Supplementing Your Child's Curriculum or Homework

You and your child have begun working together and all is well…until your child tells you that he still does not understand or you may realize that you are not really that good at teaching the skill. These are signs that tell you to supplement your child's curriculum or homework. There are several ways to do that, including hiring a tutor or searching for free online resources to help you with your child. Depending on the situation, either case will work to ensure that your child is successful with his or her studies.

### Does my child need a tutor?
Your child will only need a tutor for the subjects that you are not proficient in or comfortable teaching. Also, if your time is limited, you might hire a tutor to develop the lesson or teach your child for you.

If you choose this route with a tutor, there are a few things that you will need to consider:

1.  Why do you think that you need a tutor?

    _____

    _____

    _____

    _____

2.  In which subject(s) will your child need a tutor?

    _____

    _____

    _____

    _____

3.  How much do you have budgeted for a tutor?

    _____

    _____

    _____

    _____

4.  How often do you plan to have the tutor work with your child?

    _____

    _____

    _____

**5.** What are you looking for in a tutor?

_____

_____

_____

_____

You may be wondering why these questions are important when making a decision to hire a tutor. Here's the purpose for each question:

❏ **Question One:** You need to be kosher with your decision to hire someone else to tutor your child. You need to respect and trust that the tutor will do the job properly. Equally important, you need to allow him or her to work with your child alone. In other words, if you feel that you need to be in the same room...that's fine, but just don't say anything. Please be aware that your child may or may not open up or fully concentrate around you with another person. However, it's natural to be wary of a stranger, but just make sure you keep your distance so that your child cannot see you.

❏ **Question Two:** It is important to know which subjects your child will need assistance in and it may be a good idea to put out ads well in advance to keep quality tutors on hand. Believe it or not, good tutors go fast and are usually booked. Once you have found tutors that you like, keep a list of them. Please see the next page for an example.

## QUALIFIED TUTORS FOR [Your Child's Name]

### Math

| Name | Email Address and Phone Number | Tutoring Fee | Subjects Tutored |
|------|-------------------------------|--------------|------------------|
| Jane Doe | Jane.doe@gmail.com 555-663-0348 | $30/hr Tutor ONLY in her home | Elementary Grades Only |
| Trina Snow | dabesttutor@ yahoo.com 555-256-0728 | $45/hr includes travel fee Travel to your house | Certified in K-12 math and science. |

### All-Subjects

| Name | Email Address and Phone Number | Tutoring Fee | Subjects Tutored |
|------|-------------------------------|--------------|------------------|
| Destiny Purpose | destiny.purpose@ gmail.com 555-256-9364 | $30/hr Tutor ONLY in her home | All-subjects |
| Faith Johnson | besttutoreva@ yahoo.com 555-590-0138 | $35 hr Online Tutoring ONLY | All-subjects |

### Foreign Languages

| Name | Email Address and Phone Number | Tutoring Fee | Subjects Tutored |
|------|-------------------------------|--------------|------------------|
| Micah David | micahd@aol.com 555-256-5171 | $30/hr Travels to your home | French, Italian, German, Spanish |
| Genesis Matthew | genesis@yahoo.com | $20/hr Online via Skype | Spanish, French, African |

❏ **Question Three:** This question will help you realistically look at hiring a tutor. You will need to plan to have a tutor work with your child for at least two days.

❏ **Question Four:** If your child is extremely bright, then one day could suffice. However, you will see quicker results if you schedule two days for your child to work with the tutor.

❏ **Question Five:** This question will help you get an idea of what you are looking for in a tutor. The ideal candidate should be patient, knowledgeable, and have great interpersonal skills.

## WHERE CAN YOU FIND TUTORS?

Tutors are everywhere! The best way to find a tutor is online or through a referral from a family member, co-worker, or friend.

## WHAT ARE SOME FREE ONLINE RESOURCES TO USE AT HOME WITH YOU CHILD?

There is a myriad of online resources available to help you with your child. You will need to conduct an online search for specific resources. In this step, you have learned that you can choose to help your child on your own or you can look for help.

It's always good to look at all your options and weigh the benefits of supplementing your child's education.

> "I continue to believe that if children are given the necessary tools to succeed, they will succeed beyond their wildest dreams!"
> — David Vitter

# Step

# 6

# Assessing Your Child's Progress

At this point, do you truly know if your child understands what you have taught him or her? You may have a gut feeling, but can your child put his or her knowledge on paper? In short, you need to find out if your child is able to apply and process the information in much greater depth. In addition, you will need to assess your child to know which direction to take next in his or her academic studies.

## What types of assessments can I give my child?

There are four types of assessments that you can give your child. They are:

1. **Informal Assessments**

   Informal assessments are used to monitor your child's progress. Some examples of informal assessments

include: (a) writing samples; (b) homework; (c) journaling; and (d) discussions. Informal assessments can be used in any subject.

## 2. Performance Assessments

In this type of assessment, your child demonstrates knowledge by creating or developing a product. In Language Arts, Social Studies, and Science, it's easy to think of projects, but what about math? In math, you can have your child create projects to demonstrate knowledge.

For example, if you are teaching your child about statistics, he or she could complete a statistics project about a favorite baseball or soccer player.

## 3. Formal Assessments

Formal assessments are the paper-based assessments that most people are used to taking. Examples include state assessments, classroom assessments, and standardized testing.

You may have discovered that this type of assessment is a little bit more challenging and may not always show the full picture of your child's potential. However, it is still necessary. Formal assessments can be considered a bittersweet topic.

The bottom line is this: your child should be exposed to a variety of assessments to ensure that he or she is learning. These assessments are a great way to serve as

evidence (or documentation) that he or she can apply the skills learned.

## 4. Oral Assessments

Another informal assessment is an oral assessment. "Oral assessments are used to provide early intervention strategies, assess students' knowledge, or identify learning disabilities" (Sasson, 2009). This type of assessment can be used with any subject, but should be designed so that your child is thinking on a higher level. Oral assessments that have questions that begin with "Why" or "How" are great to use. However, you want to include questions that require basic comprehension too.

On the next few pages, you can see an example of each type of assessment. They have been created over the course of my teaching and tutoring career.

Project Due:                    Early bird points: 5 points

Name: _____

# Dr. Holland's Statistics Project

**Scatterplot:** Track the time (in minutes) that you spend completing your homework, texting, or watching TV for 10 days and create a scatterplot. Find another person that has tracked his or her time and create a scatterplot. Also, answer the following questions:

- What type of relationship is shown by each scatterplot?
- What can you conclude about the results of your scatterplot? The other person's scatterplot?

**Line Graph:** Choose a sports team (i.e. Longhorn, Aggies, and LSU) and record the overall game scores for the season. After you have found these scores, include the season year (i.e. 2009) and create a line graph to display these scores.

**Circle Graph:** Choose your favorite song (no inappropriate lyrics) and print out the lyrics. Please find out how many verbs, nouns, and adverbs are present in the song. Once you have found these parts of speech, create a table to help you

create your circle graph. Please remember that percents are when working with circle graphs.

**Stem-and-Leaf Plot:** Interview at least 35 people about the number of times that they text in an hour and record their response in a table. Using the information in the table, create a stem-and-leaf plot to display the results. Answer the following questions:

- What is the **mean, median, mode,** and **range** of the number of times people text in an hour?
- What can you conclude about the results of your stem-and-leaf plot?

**Bar Graphs and Double Bar Graphs:** Conduct a survey and ask at least 40 people a question (i.e. Do you like SpongeBob, Dora, Proud Family, or Hannah Montana?). Create a bar graph to display your results. Next, create a double bar graph using two different colors to compare the number of girls and boys who answered the survey question. (Hint: As you survey people, it would be wise to record whether they are a boy or girl).

**Line Plot:** Madea and Mr. Brown are having trouble with learning line plots. Please explain and give them an example to help them understand this concept. If you can, try to relate it in their language, as well as in a mathematical sense.

**Box and Whisker Plot:** Using a graphing calculator (in class), graph a box-and-whisker plot for each set of data. Then sketch the box-and-whisker plot. For your sketch, identify the following: **outlier, lower quartile, median, upper quartile, interquartile, range.** Last but not least, for each set of data, write a paragraph that could explain a real-life experience.

1. 46, 45, 36, 36, 52, 35, 38, 44, 53, 50, 44, 35, 37, 37
2. 7, 2, 5, 12, 13, 10, 6, 3, 4, 11, 12, 13, 10, 5, 8, 8, 9, 3, 4, 6

**Histogram:** Using the Internet, find temperatures for your birth month in the year 2009 (i.e. If you were born in March, then you would find temperatures from March 2009). Make a histogram for the data. Please be sure to add your frequency table and intervals.

**Venn diagram:** Write a problem that you could solve using a Venn diagram. Please be sure to draw the Venn diagram with labels and explain how you can solve the problem.

**Misleading Data:** Using the Internet, find a set of data about the housing market (i.e. sales, foreclosures) from 2000-2009.

1. Make a graph that gives the visual impression of a healthy housing market.
2. Make a second graph that gives the visual impression of a modest profit in sales for the housing market.
3. Compare your graphs. Which graph do you think more fairly represents the data in the table? Explain.

**Choosing an Appropriate Graph:** Write a paragraph (3-5 sentences) that explains what each graph is used for. Thus, there should be nine paragraphs in all. These graphs are the following: Venn diagram, histogram, box-and-whisker plot, line plot, line graph, double bar graph, bar graph, scatterplot, circle graph, and stem-and-leaf plot.

Rubric ID: **1394179**
## Graphing : STATISTICS PROJECT

Student Name: _____

| Category | 4 | 3 | 2 | 1 |
|---|---|---|---|---|
| Cover Page and Table of Contents | Cover page contains student name, title, course, teacher, school, and submission date. Table of contents is accurate and includes all components of the project. | One requirement is missing. | Two requirements are missing. | Three or more requirements are missing. |
| Bar Graph and Double Bar Graph | Data is well organized, accurate, and easy to read. | Data is organized, accurate, and easy to read. | Data is accurate and easy to read. | Data is not accurate and/or cannot be read. |
| Circle Graph | All data in the set is expressed in percents. There is a key to identify the different categories. | Data in the circle graph is organized, accurate, and easy to read. | Data in the circle graph is accurate and easy to read. | Data in the circle graph is not accurate and/or cannot be read. |

| Category | 4 | 3 | 2 | 1 |
|---|---|---|---|---|
| Stem-and-Leaf Plot | All data in the set is plotted correctly and in order and is easy to see. Work is neat and attractive. | All data in the set is plotted correctly and in order and is easy to see. Work is not neat (erasures or marks throughout, or the layout is such that most of the paper is not used). | Some data in the set is missing or out of order. Work is neat and attractive. | Some data in the set is missing or out of order. Work is not neat (erasures or marks throughout, or the layout is such that most of the paper is not used). |
| Histogram | It has a title. A frequency table is included. The graph is clear, neat and colorful. The x and y axis are labeled. The layout makes good use of the whole page. 100% of the calculations are correct. | One requirement is missing or 80% of the calculations are correct. Or work is not neat. | Two requirements are missing or only 70% of the calculations are correct. | Three or more requirements are missing or less than 70% of the calculations are correct. |
| Box and Whiskers Plot | It has a title and number line with labels. The graph is clear, neat, and colorful. The layout makes good use of the whole page. 100% of the calculations are correct. | One requirement is missing or only 90% of the calculations are correct. | Two requirements are missing, only 70% of the calculations are correct. Neatness is average, or the layout is such that large unused areas are present. | Four requirements are missing, less than 50% of the calculations are correct, neatness is extremely poor, or layout is such that the majority of the paper is unused. Graph fails to provide audience with any understanding. |
| Mean, Median, Mode, and Range | Has a title, which includes the name of the data set. 100% of the calculations are correct. ALL WORK is shown on the page with answers circled AND LABELED. The layout makes good use of the whole page. | One requirement is missing or only 90% of the calculations are correct. | Two requirements are missing or only 80% of the calculations are correct. | Three requirements are missing or only 70% of the calculations are correct. |

| Category | 4 | 3 | 2 | 1 |
|---|---|---|---|---|
| Line Plot | All data in the set is plotted correctly and in order and is easy to see. Work is neat and attractive. | All data in the set is plotted correctly and in order and is easy to see. Work is not neat (erasures or marks throughout, or the layout is such that most of the paper is not used). | Some data in the set is missing or out of order. Work is neat and attractive. | Some data in the set is missing or out of order. Work is not neat (erasures or marks throughout, or the layout is such that most of the paper is not used). |
| Venn Diagrams | Data is well organized, accurate, and easy to read. | Data is organized, accurate, and easy to read. | Data is accurate and easy to read. | Data is not accurate and/or cannot be read. |
| Scatter Plot | Has a title, which includes units. The x axis and y axis are labeled. All points are plotted correctly and easy to see and all questions are answered. Work is neat and attractive. | All requirements are included, but the work is not neat and attractive. | One requirement is missing or some points are excluded. Work is neat and attractive. | Two or more requirements are missing or some points are excluded and work is not neat and attractive. |
| Project Questions, Summary, and Conclusions | Is neat, has a title, is typed on a separate sheet of typing paper, uses complete sentences. Grammar and spelling are correct. ALL questions (summaries, conclusions) are included and answered thoroughly and completely in a separate paragraph that includes a topic sentence. | One requirement is missing and questions (summaries, conclusions) are well covered for audience understanding. | Two requirements are missing or questions (summaries, conclusions) are adequately covered for audience understanding. | Three requirements are missing or questions (summaries, conclusions) fail to cover material necessary for audience understanding. |

Date Created: March 25, 2007

**Adapted from www.rubistar.4teachers.org

## EXAMPLE 1: "Oral Assessment"

Please use the following questions to assess your child over the story that he or she is currently reading.

1. How did the character change in the story?
2. Identify the problem in the story.
3. Why did the author write this story?
4. Who is the protagonist? How do you know?
5. When did this story take place? Why do you think so?

## EXAMPLE 2: "Informal Assessment"

1. The weights of some award-winning fruits and vegetables are shown in the chart below.

| Item | Potato | Celery | Pumpkin | Turnip |
|---|---|---|---|---|
| Weight (lb) | $7\frac{1}{16}$ | $46\frac{1}{16}$ | $816\frac{1}{2}$ | $48\frac{3}{4}$ |
| Item | Pineapple | Onion | Garlic | Grapefruit |
| Weight (lb) | $17\frac{1}{2}$ | $10\frac{7}{8}$ | $2\frac{5}{8}$ | $3\frac{1}{8}$ |

*Source: The Guiness Book of World Records*

Explain to Mary, Grace, Lily, Paul, and Nic how to organize the fruits and vegetables into a new chart in order of weight. Please be sure to include the difference in weight between successive items.

## Can you use state-released assessments?

Absolutely! Due to the rigorousness of the assessment, this is actually preferred if you homeschool your child. On the other hand, if your child is already in school or you plan on enrolling your child in school, you should be cautious of how you use these assessments.

Most school districts use them to get an idea how students may perform on the actual state assessment. At home, your purpose is to help your child learn how to solve real-world problems. If he or she can apply the skills and learn test-taking strategies, then any assessment, including homework, should be a whole lot easier.

## Which is better? Weekly or unit tests?

You need both because you want to know how your child is performing on a weekly basis. This allows you to "catch" any misconceptions that he or she may have about the material.

In terms of unit tests, these must be given to measure your child's progress over a certain period of time.

In my opinion, both are equally important and for these assessments you should implement more than one way to assess your child.

## Where do you find assessments for your child?

- **Internet:** You can find assessments on the Internet by conducting a search for the skill that your child is currently working on.

- **Hire a Teacher to Write Assessments for you:**
  Post an ad to hire a teacher to write content for you.
  This is not expensive and you will have the satisfaction
  of knowing that your assessments are rigorous.

"It does not matter how slowly you go so long
as you do not stop."

— Confucius

*Step*

# 7

# Reporting my Child's Grades and Keeping Records

### How do I keep track of my child's growth?

There are a variety of strategies to use to keep track of your child's growth. This depends on how you want to organize the information. Let's take a look at two strategies to keep track of your child's records:

### Strategy #1: The File-Folder System

This is the most proficient way to stay organized with your child's records, especially if you are working with more than one child. Basically, the file-folder system requires you to label the subjects that you and your child are working on. I recommend using a file-folder system so that you can easily add files without the hassle of hole-punching and taking up a great deal of space in your home office.

## Strategy #2: Anecdotal Notes

During your child's lessons, you should take notes to help you remember what your child may be struggling with and where your child is doing quite well.

### Case Study:

Truth Purpose, a stay-at-home parent, decided that she would keep a notebook of her child's work because she was forgetting how her child was progressing. For one of her lessons on naming triangles according to their given angles, she wrote the following:

**Homework:** Mallorie completed her homework over triangles. She managed to finish her homework and then we started working on some test preparation for her upcoming Math test. Before Mallorie took her mini-assessment, we reviewed the various types of triangles, and how to name them according to their given angles. The Isosceles and Scalene Triangles were a bit of a challenge for Mallorie because she would make a mistake on her angle calculations. Other than that, she did a great job. Mallorie scored a 10/12, which is a 83% on TEK 6.6B.

## Expert's Advice:

Truth Purpose did herself a favor because she was able to refer back to her notes to help her child. Also, this method works because if Truth decides in the future to send her daughter to public or private school, then she has documentation and can help the school place her child in the correct grade level.

In addition, this method works for children that are already enrolled in schools. Parents can provide additional insight into that child's learning situation.

### Why is it important to keep track of my child's learning records?

If you are working with your child, you want to write down the most helpful information. For parents who homeschool, it is extremely crucial to keep records of your child's progress. For example, if you decide that your child needs a tutor, then this information can save you money and help the tutor prescribe a learning prescription for your child.

If you are helping your child at home, then this information is good to keep on file and share with your child's teachers and/or tutors.

### How do I communicate my results to my child?

Communicating results to your child is a huge task and it can determine if your child wants to continue working with you. Let's look at how this parent communicated learning results with her child:

**Case Study:**

### "TRISHA, THE INEFFECTIVE LADY"

Trisha was working with her daughter, Alivera, on dividing fractions. Her daughter completed a few homework problems and asked her mother to check them. Trisha discovered that Alivera had all of them wrong except for two problems.

Immediately, Trisha started shouting and told Alivera that she was stupid and would never get those questions right because she does not listen.

Take a moment to reflect on this situation and answer the following questions:

**1.** What did Trisha do wrong?

_____

_____

**2.** How could Trisha been more effective with her child?

_____

_____

**3.** What advice would you give to Trisha?

_____

_____


**4.** How would you respond to Alivera, if she was your child?

_____

_____


## Expert's Advice:

No matter how frustrating it may be when working with your child, you should always be positive. Trisha could have used the following:

"Alivera, I noticed that you missed a lot of your homework problems. Let's take a look at them together. How did you solve this problem?" This question could have allowed Alivera to explain her thinking and afforded Trisha the opportunity to help her child.


**"Nobody rises to low expectations."**

— Calvin Lloyd

# *Step*
# 8

# Professional Development for ME, the Parent

You may be wondering where you can improve your skills too. I would first contact local parent organizations or your child's counselor to see if there is anything available for parents in the community.

You have a great start on how to help your child at home. Best of luck and may the spirit be with you!

Should you have questions or comments for me, suggestions for future material, or tips, feel free to email me at drholland@dr-holland.com

# References

Businessballs.com (2010) Howard Gardner's Multiple Intelligences
http://www.businessballs.com/howardgardnermultiple
intelligences.htm

Dictionary.com (2010) Learning Style.
http://dictionary.reference.com/browse/learning+style

Math and Science Help (2010). Madeline Hunter's Lesson Design Model.
http://math-and-reading-help-for-kids.org/
articles/Formatting_Lesson_Plans%3A_The_Madeline_Hunter_
Lesson_Design_Model.html

MSN Encarta Dictionary (2010).
http://encarta.msn.com/dictionary_1861631837/
multiple_intelligences.html

Sasson, D. (2009). Oral diagnostic assessments for ELLs.
Retrieved November 13, 2009, from
http://esllanguageschools.suite101.com/article.cfm/oral_
diagnostic_assessments_for_ells

# About The Author

D r. Alicia Holland is one of those rare people who can say she is an educator, professional tutor, instructional designer, curriculum developer, online professor, life coach, consultant, speaker, and author and mean it. She started her teaching career at the age of 20 and later earned her doctorate degree in Education from Nova Southeastern University in Ft. Lauderdale, Florida in 2010 at the age of 26. Her God-Given talents and skills have attracted clients such as school districts throughout the United States, state agencies, and other leading learning organizations, including in the private sector.

Dr. Holland consults with tutors and other learning organizations both large and small. Her tutoring blog for tutors has been online since 2010 and she coaches tutors around the world. Typically, she speaks at major conferences each year on topics in education, including tutoring. Dr. Holland is an online associate faculty member at Concordia University

Portland where she teaches graduate courses, including doctoral level organizational leadership courses, in the School of Education.

Also, Dr. Holland has held appointments as an online professor at Ashford University, American College of Education, and Everest Online where she served in the capacity of Internship Supervisor for Bilingual and English Language Learner Educators and taught various courses in Education, Life Skills and Critical Thinking. Additionally, at Capella University, in the Graduate School of Education, she taught various courses in Education and currently serves as a Dissertation Mentor for Doctoral Learners. Lastly, Dr. Holland teaches doctoral level research courses and serve as either Dissertation Chair or Committee Member at the University of Phoenix.

When Dr. Holland is not developing new content, tutoring, teaching, or consulting with her clients, you can usually find her sight-seeing and spending quality time with her family.

CPSIA information can be obtained
at www.ICGtesting.com
Printed in the USA
LVOW04s2252161215

466800LV00017B/333/P

9 781944 346089